The Power *of*
INFLUENCE

*Devotionals of Wisdom for Being a
Positive and Powerful Influence*

RACINE, WI

The Power of Influence
ISBN: 979-8-88898-171-9 - *Paperback*
ISBN: 979-8-88898-172-6 - *Hardcover*
ISBN: 979-8-88898-173-3 - *Ebook*
Copyright © 2025 by John C. Maxwell & Honor Books, Racine, WI

INTRODUCTION

Millionaire industrialist John D. Rockefeller once said that he was willing to pay more for this ability than any other under the sun. President Theodore Roosevelt said it was the most important ingredient in the formula of success. The quality? Influence—our ability to deal with people and build positive relationships with them. More than anything else in life, relationships make or break us.

That's why it's important to keep learning about relationships and how to influence people for good. This book is designed as a short course on relationship building through positive influence. May these timeless quotes and insights from men and women who understand people help you discover and cultivate the power of influence.

JOHN C. MAXWELL

FIRST THINGS FIRST

If you're going to play together as a team, you've got to care for one another. You've got to love each other.

VINCE LOMBARDI

The Ten Commandments of Human Relations
1. Speak to people.
2. Smile at people.
3. Call people by name.
4. Be friendly and helpful.
5. Be cordial.
6. Have a genuine interest in people.
7. Be generous with praise.
8. Be considerate of the feelings of others.
9. Be thoughtful of the opinions of others.
10. Be alert to give service.

We are not human beings having a spiritual experience.
We are spiritual beings having a human experience.

PIERRE TEILHARD DE CHARDIN

Therefore encourage one another and build each other up . . .

1 THESSALONIANS 5:11 NIV

Care is a state in which something does matter; it is the source
of human tenderness.

ROLLO MAY

POWER UP

Which of these commandments is the most challenging to you?

_____

_____

_____

_____

_____

FOUR STEPS FROM IMPACT

The Law of Relationship says that every person is merely four people away from any other human on earth.

The interconnectedness of humanity is more than just a sociological marvel — it's a divine design. This "*Law of Relationship*" reminds us that we are never far from the opportunity to influence or be influenced. Every person we meet could be a bridge to someone else who needs hope, encouragement, or the love of Christ. God often moves through human connections, moments of grace through people we least expect. Treat every conversation as sacred — you may be only four people away from the person God is calling you to reach or the person He's sending to change your life.

No matter how much work you can do, no matter how engaging your personality may be, you will not advance far in business if you cannot work through others.

JOHN CRAIG

He that covereth a transgression seeketh love; but he that repeateth a matter separateth very friends.

PROVERBS 17:9

I don't know the key to success, but the key to failure is trying to please everybody.

POWER UP

Reflect on a time an unexpected connection impacted you for the better.

_____

_____

_____

_____

_____

INNATE HUMAN VALUE

You can't make the other fellow feel important in your presence if you secretly feel that he is a nobody.

LES GIBLIN

True humility begins in the heart. If we secretly view someone as less valuable, it will inevitably show—no matter how polished our words may be. But when we genuinely see others as image-bearers of God, fearfully and wonderfully made just as we are, our actions align with love. Philippians 2:3 reminds us to *"consider others better than yourselves."* To uplift others sincerely, we must first allow God to adjust our vision to see as He sees, not as the world sees. Only then can we honor others in a way that reflects the heart of Christ.

It is very easy to forgive others their mistakes; it takes more grit and gumption to forgive them for having witnessed your own.

JESSAMYN WEST

Be devoted to one another in love. Honor one another above yourselves.

ROMANS 12:10 NIV

You can't be any closer to God than you are to the person you love least.

POWER UP

Reflect on a time you misjudged someone—how have you adjusted your vision of others?

WHAT REALLY COUNTS

I n a world driven by metrics, views, and statistics, it's easy to confuse success with numbers. But heaven doesn't celebrate spreadsheets, it celebrates souls. Jesus left the ninety-nine to find the one, reminding us that people — not tallies — are what truly matter. The kingdom of God moves not through quantity but through the quality of love, compassion, and connection we extend to others. When we prioritize people over numbers, we align with God's heart and reflect His immeasurable grace.

People aren't sales resistant—they are salespeople resistant.

MARK HEBENSTREIT

Humble yourselves in the sight of the Lord,
and he shall lift you up.

JAMES 4:10

$$R + R - R = R + R$$

(Rules and Regulations minus Relationships equals
Resentment and Rebellion)

DR. DAVID SEAMANDS

POWER UP

Who in your life needs to be reminded that they count
far more than any number could?

THE SWEETNESS OF GRACE

*A drop of honey catches more flies
than a gallon of gall.*

ABRAHAM LINCOLN

I n the heat of the moment, it's our knee-jerk reactions that can often get us into trouble. Proverbs 15:1 says, *"A gentle answer turns away wrath, but a harsh word stirs up anger."* God calls us to reflect His love — not just with grand gestures, but in the small, sweet drops of encouragement, understanding, and respect. Our influence grows not by force, but by the warmth of our character.

Friendship flourishes at the fountain of forgiveness.

WILLIAM A. WARD

Forbearing one another, and forgiving one another, if any man have a quarrel against any: even as Christ forgave you, so also do ye.

COLOSSIANS 3:13

If someone hurts you, first try to figure out whether that hurt was intentional or not. Not every hurt is an attack.

POWER UP

Where can I trade bitterness for sweetness today?

THE MIRROR OF GRACE

Getting people to like you is merely the other side of liking them.

Genuine connection begins not with trying to impress, but with learning to care. When we look at others through the lens of compassion and interest — seeing their worth, listening to their stories — we often find the warmth we extend reflected back to us. Love, respect, and kindness are contagious. If you're longing to feel more connected, maybe the first step is simply to open your heart wider.

It is well to remember that the entire population of the universe with one trifling exception is composed of others.

J. A. HOLMES

Joseph found favor in his eyes and became his attendant. Potiphar put him in charge of his household, and he entrusted to his care everything he owned . . . the Lord blessed the household of the Egyptian because of Joseph.

GENESIS 39:4-5 NIV

Ninety percent of the friction of daily life is caused by the wrong tone of voice.

POWER UP

Who needs your sincere attention today?

THE WISDOM OF DISCRETION

*If you want to get along with people,
pretend you never knew whatever they tell you.*

In a culture quick to broadcast secrets and slow to guard trust, discretion has become a rare and powerful gift. Proverbs 11:13 says, *"A gossip betrays a confidence, but a trustworthy person keeps a secret."* When others feel safe confiding in us, we reflect the quiet strength of Christ, who hears much and offers kindness to us as we are. The ability to forget what doesn't need to be remembered is not deception; it's grace. Today, choose to be a safe place for others, and in doing so, draw others into the light of God.

Few things will pay you bigger dividends than the time and trouble you take to understand people. Almost nothing will add more to your stature as an executive and a person. Nothing will give you greater satisfaction or bring you more happiness.

KIENZLE AND DARE

Let not mercy and truth forsake thee: bind them about thy neck; write them upon the table of thine heart: So shalt thou find favour and good understanding in the sight of God and man.

PROVERBS 3:3-4

Each relationship nurtures a strength or weakness within you.

POWER UP

Where in your life could you grow in the wisdom of discretion?

_____

_____

_____

_____

_____

FAN THE SPARK
INTO FLAME

In God's kingdom, greatness is not measured by worldly titles, wealth, or applause—it's revealed in humility, kindness, and how we treat those who can offer us nothing in return. Jesus, the King of Kings, knelt to wash the feet of His disciples, showing us that true authority serves rather than demands. Paul tells us in 2 Timothy 1:6 to "... *fan into flame the gift of God* ..." When we listen to the unheard and lift up the lowly, we echo the heart of God and reignite the hearts of the downtrodden. Greatness isn't a spotlight we step into, but recognizing and amplifying the spark within others.

Leadership is influence.

JOHN C. MAXWELL

Do to others as you would have them do to you.

LUKE 6:31 NIV

If you want to lose friends quickly, start bagging about yourself; if you want to make and keep friends, start bagging about others.

POWER UP

Make an effort to notice someone overlooked this week —how can you lift them up?

_____

_____

_____

_____

_____

THE POWER OF THE TONGUE

*I will speak ill of no man
and speak all the good I know of everybody.*

BENJAMIN FRANKLIN

These words challenge us to rise above gossip, criticism, and negativity in a world often quick to tear down. Proverbs 18:21 says, *"The tongue has the power of life and death,"* reminding us that our words have the power to wound or heal, discourage or inspire. Choosing to speak well of others, even when it's easier to highlight their faults, is a reflection of God's grace in us. Most people battle enough negativity in their own thought lives — when we look for the good and call it out, we not only honor others but become vessels of hope and unity.

The true test of being comfortable with someone else is the ability to share silence.

FRANK TYGER

And over all these virtues put on love, which binds them all together in perfect unity.

COLOSSIANS 3:14 NIV

The man who goes alone can start the day. But he who travels with another must wait until the other is ready.

HENRY DAVID THOREAU

POWER UP

Who can you lift up with kindness today instead of criticism?

_____

_____

_____

_____

_____

FORGED IN FIRE

Relationships are not formed but forged.

Like iron shaped under intense heat and pressure, meaningful relationships are not created casually — they are built intentionally, over time, through trials, trust, and perseverance. Proverbs 27:17 reminds us, *"As iron sharpens iron, so one person sharpens another."* The bonds that endure are those that have been tested and strengthened in the fires of honesty, vulnerability, and grace. Ask God today for the strength to forge the relationships He has placed in your life with intentionality.

*The people you surround yourself with influence your be-
haviors, so choose friends who have healthy habits.*

DAN BUETTNER

*Jonathan said to David, "Go in peace, for we have sworn
friendship with each other in the name of the Lord . . .*

1 SAMUEL 20:42 NIV

*Anyone who loves his opinions more than he does his brethren
will defend his opinions and destroy his brethren.*

POWER UP

*What intentional step can you take to strengthen
or repair a relationship that came to mind today?*

OPEN HANDS, OPEN HEART

You cannot shake hands with a clenched fist.

INDIRA GANDHI

A closed hand cannot give, receive, or embrace—it only defends or resists. True connection and reconciliation are only possible when we let go of anger, pride, and need for control. Jesus calls us in Matthew 5:9, "*Blessed are the peacemakers, for they will be called children of God.*" To be peacemakers, we must first release our grip on past hurts and open ourselves to the healing work of grace. Only then can we extend a hand of peace, welcome, and unity.

*Ninety percent of the art of living consists of getting along
with people you cannot stand.*

SAMUEL GOLDWYN

*A gentle answer turns away wrath,
but a harsh word stirs up anger.*

PROVERBS 15:1 NIV

*To handle yourself, use your head.
To handle others, use your heart.*

JOHN C. MAXWELL

POWER UP

What holds you back from fully opening your heart and hands?

_____

_____

_____

_____

_____

THE PURPOSE OF TALENT

Natural talent, intelligence, a wonderful education—none of these guarantees success. Something else is needed: the sensitivity to understand what other people want and the willingness to give it to them.

JOHN LUTHER

Why does God knit and impart gifting, intelligence, and talent into us? God never does anything without purpose—He does not give individuals talent to tickle the fancy of the bearer, but to ultimately uplift others and expand His kingdom. Philippians 2:4 reminds us, *"Let each of you look not only to his own interests, but also to the interests of others."* Success in God's kingdom is measured by how we love and serve. When we cultivate empathy and generosity, we unlock doors that talent alone cannot open. Ask God today for a heart that listens and hands that respond.

This, then, is how you ought to regard us: as servants of Christ and as those entrusted with the mysteries God has revealed.

1 CORINTHIANS 4:1 NIV

Every man is entitled to be valued by his best moments.

RALPH WALDO EMERSON

Instead of putting others in their place,
put yourself in their place.

POWER UP

How do your talents play into God's call on your life?

_____

_____

_____

_____

_____

SIDE BY SIDE

*One man working with you is worth
a dozen men working for you.*

HERMAN M. KOELLIKER

R eal leadership and lasting impact are born not from command, but from collaboration. Jesus modeled this beautifully: He didn't just instruct His disciples, but He walked with them, ate with them, and served alongside them. In Galatians 6:2, we're told to *"carry each other's burdens, and in this way you will fulfill the law of Christ."* There is unmatched strength in shared purpose. When we stand shoulder to shoulder, we don't just get more done — we build something that endures. Today, look for ways to work with others, not just over them.

If you would win a man to your cause, first convince him that you are his sincere friend.

ABRAHAM LINCOLN

And whatsoever ye do, do it heartily, as to the Lord, and not unto men; Knowing that of the Lord ye shall receive the reward of the inheritance: for ye serve the Lord Christ.

COLOSSIANS 3:23-24

People don't care how much you know until they know how much you care.

JOHN C. MAXWELL

POWER UP

Who are you working alongside in this season of life?

_____

_____

_____

_____

_____

LOVE THY NEIGHBOR

The most important single ingredient in the formula of success is knowing how to get along with people.

THEODORE ROOSEVELT

As much as success is about vision, discipline, and determination, it also hinges on our ability to work alongside others. A person may be incredibly gifted and intelligent, but if one cannot get along with people, potential is stunted. Harmony, humility, and a genuine interest in others open doors that talent alone cannot. If we want to reflect Christ and make a difference in the world, we must start by valuing people the way He does. Success without love is empty, but when we honor people we reflect the heart of God.

*I will pay more for the ability to deal with people than for
any other ability under the sun.*

JOHN D. ROCKEFELLER

*The righteous choose their friends carefully, but the way of
the wicked leads them astray.*

PROVERBS 12:26 NIV

*There is a rule in sailing that the more maneuverable ship
should give way to the less maneuverable craft. I think this
is sometimes a good rule to follow in human relationships
as well.*

DR. JOYCE BROTHERS

POWER UP

*Do you know how to get along with people?
If not, how can you practice?*

A SHORT COURSE IN HUMAN RELATIONS

*A person finds joy in giving an apt reply—
and how good is a timely word!*

PROVERBS 15:23 NIV

True strength is not found in never falling short, but in owning our missteps and choosing unity over pride. Healing and growth begin when we humble ourselves, not when we pretend to be flawless. And while individual humility is vital, so is our collective identity. God designed us to live, serve, and grow in community — *we* is where love takes root and where transformation happens.

THE SIX MOST IMPORTANT WORDS:
"I admit I made a mistake."

THE FIVE MOST IMPORTANT WORDS:
"You did a good job."

THE FOUR MOST IMPORTANT WORDS:
"What is your opinion?"

THE THREE MOST IMPORTANT WORDS:
"If you please."

THE TWO MOST IMPORTANT WORDS:
"Thank you."

THE MOST IMPORTANT WORD:
"We."

THE LEAST IMPORTANT WORD:
"I."

POWER UP

*Who in your life needs an encouraging
or timely word from you today?*

_____

_____

_____

_____

_____

BREAKING THE CYCLE

> *If you are suffering from a bad man's injustice,*
> *forgive him lest there be two bad men.*
>
> AUGUSTINE

I njustice wounds deeply, tempting us to respond with bitterness or vengeance. But when we repay wrong with wrong, we mirror the very evil we despise. Jesus calls us to a higher way: *"Love your enemies and pray for those who persecute you"* (Matthew 5:44). Forgiveness doesn't excuse injustice, but it sets us free from becoming captive to it. In letting go, we refuse to let someone else's sin define our spirit. Choose grace, not grievance. Let God's mercy flow through you, and be the light that darkness cannot overcome.

Think twice before you speak, because your words and influence will plant the seed of either success or failure in the mind of another.

NAPOLEON HILL

Better is a little with righteousness than great revenues without right.

PROVERBS 16:8

Seek to be a plow rather than a bulldozer. The plow cultivates the soil, making it a good place for seed to grow. The bulldozer scrapes the earth and pushes every obstacle out of the way.

POWER UP

Who do you need to forgive?

_____

_____

_____

_____

_____

BUILDING UP ONE ANOTHER

> *Don't use your people to build a great work;*
> *use your work to build a great people.*
>
> **JACK HYLES**

Authentic leadership sees beyond goals and deadlines, it sees the God-given potential in others. Jesus didn't call disciples to accomplish a mission without also transforming their hearts. He poured into them and, through the work, made fishermen and tax-collectors into leaders and saints. Whatever role we play — teacher, parent, manager, friend — we're called not just to complete tasks, but to uplift souls. Let your labor be a tool for growth, character, and Christlike development in those around you.

Practice the one hundred and one percent principle: find one thing you agree on with another person, and then give them one hundred percent of your encouragement.

JOHN C. MAXWELL

Righteous lips are the delight of kings;
and they love him that speaketh right.

PROVERBS 16:13

You can tell more about a person by what he says about others than you can by what others say about him.

POWER UP

How can you use the work you're doing today
to encourage, grow, or uplift the people around you?

_____

_____

_____

_____

_____

A MOST NOBLE WORK

There is no more noble occupation in the world than to assist another human being—to help someone succeed.

ALAN LOY MCGINNIS

In a world that often glorifies self-promotion and individual achievement, God calls us to a higher purpose: lifting others up. Jesus modeled this perfectly, not seeking fame but stooping low to serve, teach, heal, and ultimately give His life for others. When we step aside from our own ambitions to invest in someone else's journey we reflect the heart of Christ. World-changing greatness is not found in climbing the ladder, but in holding it steady for someone else.

It is one of the most beautiful compensations of this life that no man can sincerely try to help another without helping myself.

RALPH WALDO EMERSON

Anyone who withholds kindness from a friend forsakes the fear of the Almighty.

JOB 6:14 NIV

Assets make things possible. People make things happen.

POWER UP

Think of the people in your life— who could you assist in their success and how?

THE WISDOM OF SILENCE

It is better to keep your mouth closed and let people think you are a fool than to open it and remove all doubt.

MARK TWAIN

This quote echoes the biblical truth found in Proverbs 17:28: "*Even fools are thought wise if they keep silent, and discerning if they hold their tongues.*" In a noisy world that rewards quick opinions and loud voices, God often calls us to the strength of restraint. Silence is not always weakness — it can be wisdom wrapped in humility. There are moments when our greatest witness is not what we say, but what we choose not to say. May we seek the Spirit's guidance to know when to speak truth in love, and when to quietly trust God to work without our commentary.

If you would have a happy life, remember two things: in matters of principle, stand like a rock; in matters of taste, swim with the current.

THOMAS JEFFERSON

Even a fool, when he holdeth his peace, is counted wise: and he that shutteth his lips is esteemed a man of understanding.

PROVERBS 17:28

In getting along with others, ninety-eight percent depends on our behavior with others.

POWER UP

Reflect on an instance you wish you would have kept your mouth shut. What is the cost of impulsive speech?

_____

_____

_____

_____

_____

THROUGH A PARENT'S EYES

We never know the love of our parents for us till we have become parents.

HENRY WARD BEECHER

This truth mirrors the depth of God's love for His children: an unwavering, sacrificial love we can't fully grasp until we're in the position to give it. Just as a parent wakes in the night, sacrifices time, and weathers heartache for the sake of their child, so our Heavenly Father tenderly cares for us. Jesus spoke of this kind of love when He said, *"If you then, though you are evil, know how to give good gifts to your children, how much more will your Father in heaven give good gifts to those who ask him!"* (Matthew 7:11). Today, let gratitude fill your heart—not only for your earthly parents, but for your Heavenly One, who loved you first and best.

Our minds influence the key activity of the brain, which then influences everything; perception, cognition, thoughts and feelings, personal relationships; they're all a projection of you.

DEEPAK CHOPRA

My most brilliant achievement was my ability to be able to persuade my wife to marry me.

WINSTON CHURCHILL

As a father has compassion on his children, so the Lord has compassion on those who fear him . . .

PSALM 103:13 NIV

POWER UP

How has your relationship with your earthly parents influenced your parenting? If you're not a parent, how do you imagine it would?

_____

_____

_____

_____

_____

STOKING THE FLAME

---

*Even matches made in heaven
need down-to-earth maintenance work.*

LLOYD BYERS

It's a common problem among couples outside of the newlywed stage: where has the spark gone? Even the best relationships require patience, forgiveness, communication, and consistent acts of kindness. This kind of love isn't passive and it doesn't just happen to you — it's intentional. Like any good campfire, the spark starts it, but you must feed it and stoke it. Whether in marriage, friendship, or family, don't assume love will thrive on its own. Tend to it, nurture it, and anchor it in grace. Heavenly blessings flourish best with earthly care.

*To keep the fire burning brightly, keep the two logs together,
near enough to keep each other warm, and far enough apart
—about a finger's breadth—for breathing room. Good fire,
good marriage—same rule.*

MARNIE REED CROWELL

*Two are better than one, because they have a good return for
their work: if one falls down, his friend can help him up.
But pity the man who falls and has no one to help him up!*

ECCLESIASTES 4:9-10 NIV

*God is the only third party in a marriage
that can make it work.*

POWER UP

How do you nurture love in your relationships?

_____

_____

_____

_____

_____

MIRROR OF THE HEART

Marriage is the context in which our true character is revealed. Like a mirror, it reflects our selfishness, impatience, and insecurities, but it also offers the opportunity for growth, healing, and grace. God designed marriage not to make us happy all the time, but to make us holy. As Ecclesiastes 4:9-10 reminds us, *"Two are better than one . . . If either of them falls down, one can help the other up."* Instead of blaming the bond, let us examine ourselves and let marriage be the refining fire that shapes us into the likeness of Jesus.

Let the wife make the husband glad to come home, and let him make her sorry to see him leave.

MARTIN LUTHER

Marriage is honourable in all, and the bed undefiled . . .

HEBREWS 13:4

Faith makes all things possible. Love makes all things easy. Hope makes all things work.

POWER UP

What is a new, intentional way you can invest in your marriage or closest relationship to help it grow stronger?

GRACE OVER PERFECTION

*The key to a perfect marriage is
not expecting perfection.*

In a world full of airbrushed highlight reels and fanciful rom-coms, we can easily carry unrealistic expectations into our marriages. But true love doesn't thrive in perfection, it flourishes in the climate of grace. Colossians 3:13 urges us to *"bear with each other and forgive one another if any of you has a grievance . . . Forgive as the Lord forgave you."* When we let go of the need for our spouse or ourselves to be perfect, we make room for growth, patience, and authentic love. A strong marriage is built on God-centered commitment to show up, forgive, and love the person you've chosen as your partner in life.

Love at first sight is nothing special. It's when two people have been looking at each other for years that it becomes a miracle.

SAM LEVINSON

Enjoy life with your wife, whom you love, all the days of this meaningless life that God has given you under the sun . . . For this is your lot in life and in your toilsome labor under the sun.

ECCLESIASTES 9:9 NIV

Marriage is an empty box. It remains empty unless you put in more than you take out.

POWER UP

How can you show grace instead of expecting perfection in your marriage or closest relationship this week?

_____

_____

_____

_____

_____

FROM IMPRESSIONS TO INTEGRITY

Courtship brings out the best.
Marriage brings out the rest.

CULLEN HIGHTOWER

In the early stages of love, we naturally highlight our finest qualities to leave a good impression. It's a stage many look back at with dejection, wondering why the magic hasn't translated into marriage. In the daily rhythm and deeper intimacy of marriage, parts of us that are still in need of grace, growth, and transformation are revealed. Marriage becomes a sacred space where the best and the "rest" can be met with humility, honesty, and love. When we allow God to work through our imperfections, marriage matures from impression to integrity, and love grows real and resilient.

There are two great motivators in life. One is fear. The other is love. You can lead an organization by fear, but if you do, you will ensure that people won't perform up to their real capabilities.

JAN CARLSON

If I have the gift of prophecy and can fathom all mysteries and all knowledge, and if I have a faith that can move mountains, but do not have love, I am nothing.

1 CORINTHIANS 13:2 NIV

Love will find a way. Indifference will find an excuse.

POWER UP

What can you do today to court your spouse?

BREAKING FREE

---

*The love of our neighbor is the only door
out of the dungeon of self.*

GEORGE MACDONALD

So often the narrow confines of our own needs, fears, and ambitions make us prisoners of a self-centered mindset. But Jesus calls us to something freer and far greater: sacrificial love. In Matthew 22:39, He commands, *"Love your neighbor as yourself."* It's in reaching beyond our own concerns to care for others that we experience the truest form of liberation. Selfless love breaks the chains of pride and isolation, unlocking joy, purpose, and connection. When we choose to serve, forgive, and uplift others, we find that the prison door was never locked — love was always the key.

*Genuine love is a fragile flower. It must be maintained
and protected if it is to survive. Love can perish . . . when
there is no time for romantic activity . . . when a man and
his wife forget how to talk to each other.*

JAMES DOBSON

*A new commandment I give unto you, that ye love one an-
other; as I have loved you, that ye also love one another. By
this shall all men know that ye are my disciples, if ye have
love one to another.*

JOHN 13:34-35

*Truth without love is brutality.
Love without truth is hypocrisy.*

POWER UP

*How can you step outside your own worries
and show love to someone else this week?*

LOVE COVERS

Faults are thick where love is thin.

When love is lacking, even the smallest imperfections seem enormous. Criticism replaces compassion, and judgment takes the place of grace. Love doesn't ignore faults, but it chooses to see people through the lens of mercy, not magnification. We become more patient, forgiving, and kind when others fall short if our cup is full of God's unmerited grace. Let us choose to love deeply, so grace fills the space between us and those around us.

You will find as you look back upon your life that the moments when you have really lived are the moments when you have done things in the spirit of love.

HENRY DRUMMOND

Above all, love each other deeply, because love covers over a multitude of sins.

1 PETER 4:8 NIV

The law of love always supersedes the law of personal liberty.

POWER UP

How can you choose to see others through the lens of love today, rather than focusing on faults?

THE WARM RAYS OF LOVE

Blessed is the influence of one true,
loving human soul on another.

GEORGE ELIOT

Have you ever been the recipient of a simple act of kindness on a bad day? When you've been caught up in grief or stress, the eager kindness of a stranger can part the storm clouds and remind you that hopeful, blue skies still exist. In a world aching for hope and connection, your quiet kindness, your patient presence, and your sincere love can ripple further than you'll ever see. Never underestimate the divine power of a soul surrendered to love. You may be the blessing someone's been praying for.

How far you go in life depends on your being tender with the young, compassionate with the aged, sympathetic with the striving, and tolerant of the weak and the strong. Because someday in life you will have been all of these.

GEORGE WASHINTON CARVER

The Lord is gracious, and full of compassion; slow to anger, and of great mercy.

PSALM 145:8

If you want to make your mother happy, talk to her. If you want to make your father happy, listen.

POWER UP

What influence do you hope to have on the people around you?

_____

_____

_____

_____

_____

REBUILDING THE BRIDGE

There is no lonelier person than the one who lives with a spouse with whom he or she cannot communicate.

MARGARET MEAD

When communication breaks down in a marriage, intimacy fades and loneliness moves in, even in close proximity. But God, the author of relationships, can rebuild what's been lost. Through prayer, humility, and intentional effort, He restores connection and renews understanding. Ask Him today to help you lay down pride, soften your words, and listen with love. A bridge begins with a single plank of honest, grace-filled conversation.

When I'm getting ready to reason with a man, I spend one-third of my time thinking about myself and what I am going to say—and two-thirds thinking about him and what he is going to say.

ABRAHAM LINCOLN

Instead, speaking the truth in love, we will grow to become in every respect the mature body of him who is the head, that is, Christ.

EPHESIANS 4:15 NIV

A man should choose of his wife the woman he would choose as his best friend, were she a man.

POWER UP

Do you consider yourself a good communicator? Where could you improve?

_____

_____

_____

_____

_____

WALLS OF HURT

---

*People are lonely because they build walls
instead of bridges.*

JOSEPH F. NEWTON

I t's a truth we often ignore: the very defenses
we raise to protect ourselves can become
the barriers that isolate us. God created us
for connection, not isolation, and calls us to love
one another deeply and sincerely. Healing and community begin when we reach out. Today, let the love
of Christ empower you to dismantle those walls
and start building bridges.

To keep your marriage brimming
With love in the loving cup,
When you're wrong, admit it.
When you're right, shut up.

OGDEN NASH

Let your speech be always with grace, seasoned with salt,
that ye may know how ye ought to answer every man.

COLOSSIANS 4:6

It's when you rub elbows with a man that you find out what
he has up his sleeve.

POWER UP

Have you built up any walls in your life?

_____

_____

_____

_____

_____

THE DIVINE TRIANGLE

*Successful marriage is always a triangle:
a man, a woman, and God.*

CECIL MYERS

At the center of every thriving marriage is not just love between two people, but a shared connection with the One who is Love Himself. When God is the apex of the relationship triangle, He draws both hearts closer to Him — and in doing so, closer to each other. This divine bond provides strength during trials, grace during conflict, and joy in the journey. *"A cord of three strands is not quickly broken"* (Ecclesiastes 4:12). Invite God into your relationship daily — not as a guest, but as the foundation. A marriage rooted in Him has the power not only to endure but to flourish.

Train up a child in the way he should go—and walk there yourself once in a while.

JOSH BILLINGS

Train up a child in the way he should go: and when he is old, he will not depart from it.

PROVERBS 22:6

Parents are prone to give their children everything except the one thing they need most. That is time.

EMMA K. HULBURT

POWER UP

What is one intentional way you can invite God into your marriage or relationship today to strengthen that sacred triangle?

_____

_____

_____

_____

_____

FEARFULLY AND WONDERFULLY MADE

*Never try to make your son or daughter
another you; one is enough!*

ARNOLD GLASOW

As parents, it's tempting to mold our children in our own image, hoping they follow the paths we've paved. But God, in His infinite creativity, designed each child uniquely with their own calling, gifts, and identity. Our greatest role is not to clone ourselves, but to cultivate who God created them to be. By letting go of the pressure to replicate our journey, we give them the freedom to walk confidently in theirs — entrusting God as their guide and us as their cheerleaders.

The most important thing that parents can teach their children is how to get along without them.

FRANK A. CLARK

Children are a heritage from the Lord, offspring a reward from him. Like arrows in the hands of a warrior are children born in one's youth.

PSALM 127:3–4 NIV

If there is anything better than being loved, it loving.

POWER UP

How can you encourage your child to embrace their unique God-given identity today, instead of shaping them in your image?

THE GIFT OF PRESENCE

The best gift a father can give to his son
is the gift of himself—his time.

C. NEIL STRAIT

Most parents have shaken their heads at an expensive toy or gift, eagerly and emphatically desired by their child for Christmas, cast aside weeks or even days later. Children won't remember the lavish gifts, they'll remember your presence or lack thereof. Just as our Heavenly Father is always near, never too busy to listen or love, we too are called to reflect that divine availability. Time spent with our children becomes the soil in which trust, identity, and faith take root. Fathers, your time isn't just a gift; it's a legacy.

There is no more lovely, friendly, and charming relationship, communion, or company than a good marriage.

MARTIN LUTHER

I was young and now I am old, yet I have never seen the righteous forsaken or their children begging bread. They are always generous and lend freely; their children will be a blessing.

PSALM 37:25-26 NIV

By the time we realize our parents may have been right, we usually have children who think we are wrong.

POWER UP

Do you have dedicated time with your kids each week? If not, how much can you practically carve out?

CHOSEN COMPANIONS

God chooses our relatives; we choose our friends.

While family is a divine assignment, friendship is a sacred selection. Proverbs 18:24 tells us, *"There is a friend who sticks closer than a brother,"* reminding us that friendships, when rooted in Christ, can carry us through life's greatest joys and deepest valleys. The friends we choose shape our character, direct our steps, and influence our hearts. Choose wisely — select those who encourage your faith, challenge your growth, and walk with you toward God's purposes.

The formula for achieving a successful relationship is simple: you should treat all disasters as if they were trivialities, but never treat a triviality as if it were a disaster.

QUENTIN CRISP

Both the one who makes people holy and those who are made holy are of the same family. So Jesus is not ashamed to call them brothers and sisters.

HEBREWS 2:11 NIV

Never be yoked to one who refuses the yoke of Christ.

POWER UP

How have your chosen companions enriched your life? Consider encouraging them by telling them what you write here.

THE ART OF LISTENING

To listen well is as powerful a means of communication and influence as to talk well.

JOHN MARSHALL

In our social media age, where many rush to share their thoughts and opinions, truly listening is a lost art. James 1:19 reminds us, *"Everyone should be quick to listen, slow to speak and slow to become angry."* When we listen with our whole hearts, we offer others compassion, validation, and love. Jesus modeled this beautifully, often pausing to hear the cries of the hurting before He healed or helped. Listening opens the door to deeper relationships, clearer understanding, and the kind of influence that leaves a lasting mark.

A gossip is one who talks to you about others; a bore is one who talks to you about himself; and a brilliant conversationalist is one who talks to you about yourself.

LISA KIRK

A man that hath friends must shew himself friendly: and there is a friend that sticketh closer than a brother.

PROVERBS 18:24

Most communication problems can be solved with proximity.

POWER UP

Who in your life can you offer a compassionate ear?

_____

_____

_____

_____

_____

A GLIMPSE OF HEAVEN

A friend is a person with whom I may be sincere.
Before him, I may think aloud.

RALPH WALDO EMERSON

What a rare and precious gift it is to have someone in our lives before whom we can lay down our guard and simply be ourselves. True friendship reflects the heart of God as a safe space where authenticity is welcomed and burdens are shared. When we find such a friend, or become one, we begin to embody God's kingdom on Earth as it is in heaven. Let us cherish and nurture these bonds, and thank God for the people who allow us to be fully known and fully loved.

The opinions which we hold of one another, our relationships with friends and kinsfolk are in no sense permanent, save in appearance, but are as eternally fluid as the sea itself.

MARCEL PROUST

Each of you should use whatever gift you have received to serve others, as faithful stewards of God's grace in its various forms.

1 PETER 4:10 NIV

The harder you work at relationship, the harder it is to surrender.

POWER UP

Who is a friend you can be real with today and how can you create space for them to be real with you?

_____

_____

_____

_____

_____

THE COMPANY YOU KEEP

> *A man is known by the company he organizes.*
>
> AMBROSE PIERCE

Who we choose to surround ourselves with and what we build together says more about us than words ever could. Scripture reminds us in Proverbs 13:20, *"Walk with the wise and become wise, for a companion of fools suffers harm."* The people we align ourselves with often reflect the values we hold deepest. Whether in business, ministry, friendship, or family, we are constantly forming a kind of "company" that speaks to our character and can influence everything from our attitudes to our very future. Ponder your inner circle and either celebrate those you've bonded with or reconsider the foundations of those connections.

*A wise man associating with the vicious becomes an idiot;
a dog traveling with good men becomes a rational being.*

ARABIC PROVERB

*Go from the presence of a foolish man, when thou perceivest
not in him the lips of knowledge.*

PROVERBS 14:7

*You will acquire the vices and virtues of your closest asso-
ciates. The fragrance of their lives will pervade your life.*

JOHN C. MAXWELL

POWER UP

What does your circle of friends say about you?

THE SHAPE OF INFLUENCE

Tell me thy company, and I'll tell thee what thou art.

CERVANTES

J ust as iron sharpens iron, the right companions challenge, inspire, and refine us into who
God is calling us to be. In a similar way, some
friendships are more like sandpaper to wood, wear-
ing away your peace of mind and godly character
into dust. Abrasion in itself isn't bad. It's needed for
sharpening, but it can also dull your edge. Don't shy
away from challenging relationships, but be mind-
ful of how they are shaping you.

Every man is like the company he is wants to keep.

EURIPIDES

Do not be misled: "Bad company corrupts good character."

1 CORINTHIANS 15:33 NIV

In choosing a friend, go up a step.

JEWISH PROVERB

POWER UP

How have your friendships shaped you over the years?

_____

_____

_____

_____

_____

WHO ARE YOU LIVING FOR?

Standing firm in truth often makes us stand out and not always in flattering ways. When you walk with God's wisdom, you may appear out of step with the world, but you are in rhythm with heaven. Don't let mockery or misunderstanding shake your confidence — remember whose opinion will trump all the others. Wisdom is not always celebrated in the moment, but it is always honored by God. Stay faithful, even if you look foolish doing it, because of who you are doing it for!

He that lies down with dogs shall rise up with flies.

LATIN PROVERB

He that walketh with wise men shall be wise:
but a companion of fools shall be destroyed.

PROVERBS 13:20

It is better to weep with wise men than to laugh with fools.

SPANISH PROVERB

POWER UP

Reflect on a time standing by your values reaped momentary
humiliation, but long-term wisdom?

_____

_____

_____

_____

_____

BURDENS WE CANNOT SEE

No one knows the weight of another's burden.

THOMAS FULLER

Many of us have been there: attempting to go about our day while carrying invisible pain, silent struggle, or deep sorrow. Every one is carrying something, especially those who don't know the hope of Jesus. As followers of Christ, we are called to embody compassion and humility — offering kindness, not criticism; patience, not pressure. Galatians 6:2 says, *"Carry each other's burdens, and in this way you will fulfill the law of Christ."* Be the person you needed at your darkest time and extend grace to others.

Just as much as we see in others we have in ourselves.

WILLIAM HAZLITT

A friend loves at all times, and a brother is born for a time of adversity.

PROVERBS 17:17 NIV

Most often it happens that one attributes to others only the feelings of which one is capable oneself.

ANDRÉ GIDE

POWER UP

What kindness from another would have made a world of a difference to you at your darkest moments? How can you be that for others?

_____

_____

_____

_____

_____

OUR FELLOW MAN

> *The longer we live, the more we find*
> *we are like other persons.*
>
> OLIVER WENDELL HOLMES

Time has a way of humbling us, revealing that we all wrestle with similar fears, hopes, and longings beneath the surface. This truth invites us to look at others not with suspicion or superiority, but with empathy. When we see our shared humanity, we stop competing and start connecting. Today, ask God to help you embrace the common thread He has woven into each of us and let it shape how you love those around you.

Hurting people hurt people.

JOHN C. MAXWELL

*Let another man praise thee, and no thine own mouth;
a stranger, and not thine own lips.*

PROVERBS 27:2

*No man is much pleased with a companion who does not
increase, in some respect, his fondness of himself.*

SAMUEL JOHNSON

POWER UP

How can you find common ground with someone today?

_____

_____

_____

_____

_____

BEYOND THE SURFACE

> *One learns people through the heart,*
> *not the eyes or the intellect.*
>
> **MARK TWAIN**

T rue understanding of others doesn't come from outward appearances or clever analysis — it comes from a heart willing to listen and care. When God looks at us, He sees beyond our actions and words to the core of who we are. 1 Samuel 16:7 says, "*The Lord does not look at the things people look at . . . the Lord looks at the heart.*" If we want to love like Jesus, we must move beyond judgments and open our hearts to truly know and walk with others.

Don't drown the man who taught you to swim. If you learned your trade or profession from the man, do not set up in opposition to him.

C. H. SPURGEON

My command is this: Love each other as I have loved you.

JOHN 15:12 NIV

Love or perish.

POWER UP

How do you learn people? Are your findings accurate?

_____

_____

_____

_____

_____

THE HEART OF THE FATHER

It is wise father that knows his own child.

SHAKESPEARE

This ancient truth echoes God's model of fatherhood: deeply present, endlessly patient, and intimately aware of His children's hearts. A wise father doesn't just provide and discipline — he studies his child, learning their dreams, struggles, and strengths. Just as our Heavenly Father knows us completely, earthly fathers are called to reflect that same attentiveness and love. With a world full of options to distract, the greatest gift a father can give is the intentional pursuit of his child's heart. Wisdom begins with presence — and love that listens.

*What the mother sings to the cradle
goes all the way down to the coffin.*

HENRY WARD BEECHER

*Children's children are the crown of old men;
and the glory of children are their fathers.*

PROVERBS 17:6

*It is the atmosphere created primarily by the mother
that makes a home worthwhile.*

J. R. BOOKHOFF

POWER UP

*In what ways has your relationship as a child of God
influenced your parenting?*

_____

_____

_____

_____

_____

THE BANK OF A FATHER'S LOVE

A father is a banker provided by nature.

FRENCH PROVERB

The deeper truth lies in the father's role as a reservoir of strength, support, and sacrifice. Like a banker manages resources, a godly father invests his time, energy, and love into the lives of his children—often at great personal cost. He provides not only for physical needs but for emotional and spiritual ones as well. As Philippians 4:19 reminds us, God supplies all our needs, and fathers reflect this divine provision when they give of themselves without counting the cost.

You don't have to deserve your mother's love. You have to deserve your father's. He's more particular.

ROBERT FROST

And my God will meet all your needs according to the riches of his glory in Christ Jesus.

PHILIPPIANS 4:19 NIV

Where parents do too much for their children, the children will not do much for themselves.

ELBERT HUBBARD

POWER UP

In what ways can you invest in your child's life today?

_____

_____

_____

_____

_____

THE COST OF ANGER

An angry father is most cruel toward himself.

PUBLILIUS SYRUS

Though anger may seem directed at others, its deepest wound often strikes the one who carries it. For fathers especially, unchecked anger can fracture relationships, rob peace, and reap regret. James 1:20 reminds us, "*Human anger does not produce the righteousness that God desires.*" A father's true strength is found not in harsh words or raised voices, but in self-control, patience, and love that mirrors the heart of our Heavenly Father. When anger rises, let grace rise higher.

*Every child comes with the message that God
is not yet discouraged of man.*

RABINDRANATH TAGORE

*And, ye fathers, provoke not your children to wrath: but bring
them up in the nurture and admonition of the Lord.*

EPHESIANS 6:4

*Romance fails us and so do friendships, but the relationships
of parent and child, less noisy than all others, remains in-
delible and indestructible, the strongest relationship on earth.*

THEODORE REIK

POWER UP

How do you deal with anger?

RARE BUT REAL

> *There is scarcity of friendship, but not of friends.*
>
> THOMAS FULLER

In a world overflowing with acquaintances, true friendship remains a rare treasure. Many may fill our social circles, but only a few earn the title of confidant, encourager, or soul companion. Let us not settle for surface connections, but pray for—and strive to be—the kind of friend who reflects Christ: faithful, selfless, and present. True friendship is scarce, but when found, it's priceless.

Acquaintance, n. A person whom we know well enough to borrow from, but not well enough to lend to.

AMBROSE PIERCE

Ointment and perfume rejoice the heart: so doth the sweetness of a man's friend by hearty counsel.

PROVERBS 27:9

A companion loves some agreeable qualities which a man may possess, but a friend loves the man himself.

JAMES BOSWELL

POWER UP

What intentional step can you take this week to deepen a friendship?

_____

_____

_____

_____

_____

THE GATEWAY TO PEACE

It is by forgiving that one is forgiven.

MOTHER TERESA

F orgiveness is not only a gift we give others, it's a key that unlocks freedom for ourselves. Jesus taught us in Matthew 6:14, *"For if you forgive other people when they sin against you, your heavenly Father will also forgive you."* Harboring bitterness only chains our hearts to pain, but releasing others through grace opens our lives to the same mercy God so freely offers us. Forgiveness is hard, but it is holy. When we extend it, we reflect the very heart of Christ—and step into the abundant peace He promises.

A man should keep his friendship in constant repair.

SAMUEL JOHNSON

He has shown you, O mortal, what is good. And what does the Lord require of you? To act justly and to love mercy and to walk humbly with your God.

MICAH 6:8 NIV

Forsake not an old friend, for a new one does not compare with him.

THE APOCRYPHA

POWER UP

Take a moment to reflect—are you harboring any offense towards another? What would it take to let it go?

_____

_____

_____

_____

_____

FRIENDSHIP OVER FAIRNESS

Between friends there is no need of justice.

ARISTOTLE

T rue friendship is built not on strict fairness but on grace, love, and understanding. In real relationships, we don't keep score — we offer patience, forgiveness, and support, even when it isn't deserved. Proverbs 17:17 reminds us, "*A friend loves at all times*," meaning that love goes beyond what is fair or expected. The foundation of friendship reflects God's own heart toward us: He doesn't deal with us as our sins deserve but covers us with mercy. Be the kind of friend who chooses grace over keeping score, and watch how God deepens the bonds that truly matter.

*Of all the things granted by wisdom, none is greater
or better than friendship.*

PIETRO ARETINO

*After Job had prayed for his friends, the Lord restored his
fortunes and gave him twice as much as he had before.*

JOB 42:10 NIV

*Friendship is a strong habitual inclination in two persons
to promote the good and happiness of one another.*

EUSTACE BUDGELL

POWER UP

*Do your closest friendships reflect grace and understanding,
or are you keeping score?*

_____

_____

_____

_____

_____

WORTH THE WAIT

*Wishing to be friends is quick work,
but friendship is a slow-ripening fruit.*

ARISTOTLE

True friendship remains a process that cannot be rushed, in a culture of instant connections. It takes time, trust, shared trials, and grace to grow something deep and lasting. Like fruit ripening in its season, genuine friendship develops with patience and intentional care. Don't be discouraged if relationships take time to deepen. The sweetest bonds are those cultivated slowly, watered with honesty, and nourished by loyalty. Good things grow in God's time—friendship included.

*The firmest friendships have been formed in mutual adversity,
as iron is most strongly united by the fiercest flame.*

CHARLES CALEB COLTON

*Faithful are the wounds of a friend;
but the kisses of an enemy are deceitful.*

PROVERBS 27:6

*The greatest ability in business is to get along with others
and to influence their actions.*

JOHN HANCOCK

POWER UP

What fruits of friendship are most valuable to you?

_____

_____

_____

_____

_____

YOU DON'T KNOW WHAT YOU'VE GOT 'TIL IT'S GONE

True friendship is like sound health—
the value of it is seldom known until it be lost.

CHARLES CALEB COLTON

So often we take for granted the steady presence of a faithful friend, much like we overlook the quiet gift of good health. Yet when that friendship is strained or lost, we suddenly feel the ache of its absence. Cherish the friends God has placed in your life. Don't wait until distance or difficulty makes you realize how vital they are—thank God for them today, and be the kind of friend you'd never want to lose.

*Friendship makes prosperity more brilliant
and lightens adversity by dividing and sharing it.*

CICERO

*He that walketh with wise men shall be wise:
but a companion of fools shall be destroyed.*

PROVERBS 13:20

*The friendships which last are those wherein each friend
respects the other's dignity to the point of not really wanting
anything from him.*

CYRIL CONNOLLY

POWER UP

How can you savor the friendships you have in this season of life?

A RARE BOND

David and Jonathan, whose bond is recorded in Scripture, is an example of deep, godly friendship between men. 1 Samuel 18:1 says, *"The soul of Jonathan was knit to the soul of David, and Jonathan loved him as his own soul."* True friendships stand the test of trials, time, and differences. They are gifts from God that reflect His love and faithfulness. If you have such a friend, cherish them! Strive to be one yourself, for in doing so, your life may quietly echo the kind of rare love that heaven honors.

It is one of the blessings of old friends that you can afford to be stupid with them.

RALPH WALDO EMERSON

My intercessor is my friend as my eyes pour out tears to God; on behalf of a man he pleads with God as one pleads for a friend.

JOB 16:20-21 NIV

Real friendship is shown in times of trouble; prosperity is full of friends.

EURIPIDES

POWER UP

What needs to change for deep friendship to flourish among men?

_____

_____

_____

_____

_____

TO FIND A FRIEND, BE A FRIEND

> *The only way to have a friend is to be one.*
>
> RALPH WALDO EMERSON

We often long for deep, meaningful friendships, yet are unaware or unwilling to invest to the time and effort it takes to attain them. God's design reminds us that love, encouragement, and loyalty must flow from us before they return to us. Proverbs 18:24 says, *"A man who has friends must himself be friendly."* True friendship begins with intentional kindness, honesty, and a willingness to invest in others without expecting immediate returns. If you desire strong, lasting relationships, start by sowing the seeds—be present, listen well, forgive often, and love selflessly.

One loyal friend is worth ten thousand relatives.

EURIPIDES

Offer hospitality to one another without grumbling.

1 PETER 4:9 NIV

The more tranquil a man becomes, the greater is his success, his influence, his power for good. Calmness of mind is one of the beautiful jewels of wisdom.

JAMES ALLEN

POWER UP

What is your strength as a friend?

_____

_____

_____

_____

_____

FAMILY WE CHOOSE

A good friend is my nearest relation.

THOMAS FULLER

While family connects us by blood, true friendship binds us by choice, love, and shared journey. Sometimes where family fails, God brings people into our lives who become our chosen family. These are the people who lift us when we fall, challenge us when we stray, and cheer us on when we grow weary. Never underestimate the sacred gift of a good friend—they are God's reminder that love knows no limits of bloodline or background.

Friendship multiplies the good of life and divides the evil.

BALTASAR GRACIÁN

When Job's three friends . . . heard about all the troubles that had come upon him, they set out from their homes and met together by agreement to go and sympathize with him and comfort him.

JOB 2:11 NIV

A friend may well be reckoned the masterpiece of nature.

RALPH WALDO EMERSON

POWER UP

What friend in your life has made you feel like family, and how do you echo that in your own life?

THE COMFORT OF A FRIEND

A sympathetic friend can be quite as dear as a brother.

HOMER

I n life's hardships, it is often the gentle presence of a friend who comforts, encourages, and reminds us we are not alone. Jesus speaks in Matthew 5:4, *"Blessed are those who mourn, for they will be comforted."* The comfort of God can manifest itself in a variety of ways—the sympathy of a friend reflects the heart of Christ, who never leaves us in our sorrow. Treasure those friendships —they are heaven's reminder that family can be found in unexpected places.

*Your friend is a man who knows all about you,
and still likes you.*

ELBERT HUBBARD

*Make no friendship with an angry man; and with a furi-
ous man thou shalt not go: lest thou learn his ways, and get
a snare to thy soul.*

PROVERBS 22:24-25

Love is rarer than genius itself. And friendship is rarer still.

CHARLES PÉGUY

POWER UP

*Reflect on a instance a friend provided comfort to you when you most
needed it. How has that kindness shaped you?*

_____

_____

_____

_____

_____

THE BLESSING OF A TRUE FRIEND

A true friend is the greatest of all blessings.

FRANÇOIS LA ROCHEFOUCAULD

A true friend really is one of life's greatest blessings. In a world full of quick and casual connections, having someone who has chosen to truly know you, encourage you, and walk beside you is priceless. Proverbs 27:9 reminds us, *"The sweetness of a friend comes from their heartfelt advice."* Real friends celebrate with us when life is good and lift us up when life gets hard. They're one of the ways God shows His love in everyday moments.

Hold a true friend with both your hands.

NIGERIAN PROVERBS

Elijah said to Elisha, "Stay here; the Lord has sent me to Bethel." But Elisha said, "As surely as the Lord lives and as you live, I will not leave you." So they went down to Bethel.

2 KINGS 2:2 NIV

The proper office of a friend is to side with you when you are in the wrong. Nearly anybody will side with you when you are in the right.

MARK TWAIN

POWER UP

How can you be true in your friendship this week?

_____

_____

_____

_____

_____

EQUALITY & FRIENDSHIP

Friendship either finds or makes equals.

PUBLILIUS SYRUS

Isn't it amazing how true friendship has a way of leveling the playing field? No matter our background, status, or differences, real friends meet heart-to-heart. It's not about who's more successful, more talented, or has life all figured out—it's about showing up for each other with honesty, care, and respect. Romans 12:16 reminds us, "*Live in harmony with one another. Do not be proud, but be willing to associate with people of low position.*" True friendship isn't impressed by titles—it's built on love that sees the heart.

A man cannot be said to succeed in this life
who does not satisfy one friend.

HENRY DAVID THOREAU

They devoted themselves to the apostles' teaching and to
fellowship, to the breaking of bread and to prayer. All the
believers were together and had everything in common.

ACTS 2:42,44 NIV

You cannot be friends upon any other terms than upon the
terms of equality.

WOODROW WILSON

POWER UP

Are you showing up as an equal in your closest friendships,
giving as much support, trust, and honesty as you hope to receive?

WHAT YOUR LIFE SPEAKS

You can never really live anyone else's life, not even your child's. The influence you exert is through your own life, and what you've become yourself.

ELEANOR ROOSEVELT

It's easy to want to guide the people we love, especially our kids, by steering their choices or protecting them from every wrong turn. But the truth is, the biggest influence we'll ever have is simply the example of life we live every day. Our words matter, but our actions speak louder — how we handle stress, how we show love, how we stay faithful. Want to influence someone's life for the better? Start by living yours with purpose, grace, and integrity — the rest will follow.

Let us be grateful to people who make us happy, they are the charming gardeners who make our souls blossom.

MARCEL PROUST

. . . set an example for the believers in speech, in conduct, in love, in faith and in purity.

1 TIMOTHY 4:12 NIV

There is no influence like the influence of habit.

GILBERT PARKER

POWER UP

What does the substance of your life speak of?

THE SWEETNESS OF LIFE

*Friendship is unnecessary, like philosophy, like art . . .
It has no survival value; rather it is one of those things
that give value to survival.*

C. S. LEWIS

Food, water, shelter — these are the basics to human survival. Simply making ends meet to live another day is the unfortunate reality for many across the globe. But we were created to thrive, not simply survive. God created us for connection, for joy, for those unexpected moments when a friend's encouragement or laughter lifts the weight of the day. Life is more than just making it through. Friendship and gratitude fills life with meaning, no matter your tax bracket.

*Only a person who has faith in himself
is able to be faithful to others.*

ERICH FROMM

*Love is patient, love is kind. It does not envy, it does not boast,
it is not proud. It does not dishonor others, it is not self-
seeking, it is not easily angered, it keeps no record of wrongs.*

1 CORINTHIANS 13:4-5 NIV

You cannot antagonize and influence at the same time.

JOHN KNOX

POWER UP

*What joy and value has the sweetness of friendship
brought to your life?*

_____

_____

_____

_____

_____

JOY IN GIVING

There is more pleasure in loving than being beloved.

THOMAS FULLER

I t's easy to want love and appreciation from others, but the real surprise comes when we discover there's actually more joy in loving others than in being loved ourselves. Thomas Fuller's words echo what Jesus taught in Acts 20:35: *"It is more blessed to give than to receive."* Loving freely, without strings attached, reflects God's heart and brings a deep joy that outlasts the ups and downs of life.

We should measure affection, not like youngsters by the ardor of our passion, but by its strength and constancy.

CICERO

Love does not delight in evil but rejoices with the truth. It always protects, always trusts, always hopes, always perseveres.

1 CORINTHIANS 13:6-7 NIV

By a great man, however, we mean a man who, because of his spiritual gifts, his character, and other qualities, deserves to be called great and who as a result earns the power to influence others.

FREDRIK BAJER

POWER UP

Do you find joy in giving love freely, or are you waiting to be loved first? What might change if you led with love?

QUICK TO LISTEN, SLOW TO SPEAK

Give every man thine ear, but few thy voice.

SHAKESPEARE

Shakespeare relays wisdom here that is echoed throughout scripture. When we slow down, listen with our hearts, and speak with thoughtfulness, we build trust, show respect, and mirror God's character. You don't have to have all the answers—sometimes the greatest gift you can offer someone is simply your ear. Let these truths sink into your soul and watch how God uses your quiet presence to make a difference.

Most Americans don't, in any vital sense, get together;
they only do things together.

LOUIS KRONBERGER

One who loves a pure heart and who speaks with grace will
have the king for a friend.

PROVERBS 22:11 NIV

Never speak of yourself to others; make them talk about them-
selves instead: therein lies the whole art of pleasing. Every
knows it and everyone forgets it.

EDMOND AND JULES DE GONCOURT

POWER UP

How accessible is you ear to others?

STRENGTH IN NUMBERS

> *A single arrow is easily broken,*
> *but not ten in a bundle.*
>
> **JAPANESE PROVERB**

Anyone who has been through hard times knows how much power there is in the loving offer of a helping hand. If you're a loner stuck in your ways, it can be difficult to accept support, even when you desperately need it. But God designed us for community, to lift each other up and share the load. Ecclesiastes 4:12 reminds us, *"Though one may be overpowered, two can defend themselves. A cord of three strands is not quickly broken."* Lean on your people, let them lean on you, and watch how God weaves your lives together for strength you could never have on your own.

The holy passion of friendship is so sweet and steady and loyal and enduring in nature that it will last through a whole lifetime, if not asked to lend money.

MARK TWAIN

Behold, how good and how pleasant it is for brethren to dwell together in unity!

PSALM 133:1

Friendship improves happiness and abates misery, by the doubling of our joy and the dividing of our grief.

MARCUS TULLIUS CICERO

POWER UP

Are you walking through life alone when God may be calling you to lean into community for strength and support?

LOVE: A MIRACLE

L ove is a miracle. Anyone who has fallen in love or become a parent knows the magic. That's because real love—whether it's for God, for people, or for the dreams He's planted in our hearts—fills us with hope that goes beyond logic. Jesus encourages us in Mark 10:27, *"With man this is impossible, but not with God; all things are possible with God."* When love leads the way, suddenly mountains don't seem so unmovable and obstacles don't seem so final. Love gives us courage to keep believing, even when it's hard.

Love means giving one's self to another person fully, not just physically. When two people really love each other, this helps them to stay alive and grow. One must really be loved to grow.

NANCY REAGAN

Many waters cannot quench love, neither can the floods drown it.

SONG OF SOLOMON 8:7

A friend is someone who gives you total freedom to be yourself.

JIM MORRISON

POWER UP

What miracles of love have you experienced in your life?

LOVE IS A SACRIFICE

Love is the true price of love.

GEORGE HERBERT

I t sounds simple, but it's real. Love always costs something. Whether it's our time, our patience, our comfort zone, or the choice to show up when it's hard, love isn't free. But here's the beautiful part: the more we give it, the more it grows. Jesus showed us that love isn't about keeping score, it's about pouring ourselves out for others, just like He did for us. 1 John 4:19 reminds us, *"We love because He first loved us."* Loving people may stretch you, but it's also the richest, most rewarding thing you'll ever invest in.

The course of love never did run smooth.

SHAKESPEARE

Greater love hath no man than this, that a man lay down his life for his friends.

JOHN 15:13

Be slow to fall into friendship; but when thou art in, continue firm and constant.

SOCRATES

POWER UP

Reflect on an instance you benefited from the sacrificial love of another. How has this influenced how you love?

_____

_____

_____

_____

_____

GUIDANCE VS. MANIPULATION

Parenting is a wild ride. We want to guide our kids, protect them, and help them make wise choices, but sometimes the best advice starts with simply listening. Proverbs 20:5 says, "*The purposes of a person's heart are deep waters, but one who has insight draws them out.*" When we listen first, we open the door for real influence. Take time to hear your child's heart—you might be surprised how easily your guidance lines up with what's already stirring in them.

If you've never been hated by your child,
you've never been a parent.

BETTE DAVIS

Listen to advice and accept discipline, and at the end you will
be counted among the wise.

PROVERBS 19:20 NIV

I talk and talk, and I haven't taught people in fifty years
what my father taught by example in one week.

MARIO CUOMO

POWER UP

Are you truly listening to your child's heart and dreams,
or are you guiding them based on your own hopes and fears?

LOVE OVERFLOWS

One of the greatest gifts a dad can give his kids isn't a toy, a trip, or even words of advice—it's loving their mom well. When kids see love, respect, and kindness in action between their parents, it builds security deep in their hearts. It teaches them what love looks like and what they deserve in their own relationships one day. Ephesians 5:25 reminds us, "*Husbands, love your wives, just as Christ loved the church.*" That kind of love is steady, selfless, and strong—and it overflows into the whole family.

*Every generation revolts against its fathers
and makes friends with its grandfathers.*

LEWIS MUMFORD

Husbands, love your wives, and be not bitter against them.

COLOSSIANS 3:19

*Build me a son, O Lord, who will be strong enough to know
when he is weak, and brave enough to face himself when
he is afraid, one who will be proud and unbending in honest defeat, and humble and gentle in victory.*

PRAYER OF DOUGLAS MACARTHUR

POWER UP

*What does your love for your spouse or closest relationship
display about you?*

UNCONDITIONAL LOVE

The depth of the love of parents for their children cannot be measured. It is like no other relationship. It exceeds concern for life itself. The love of a parent for a child is continuous and transcends heartbreak and disappointment.

JAMES E. FAUST

There's no love quite like the love a parent has for their child. It's a glimpse into God's love for us—a love that never gives up, never runs dry, and never depends on our perfection. Psalm 103:13 says, *"As a father has compassion on his children, so the Lord has compassion on those who fear him."* Parents reflect that same steady, unconditional love to their kids, holding space for grace even in the hard moments. If you're a parent, know this: your love makes a difference. And if you've been on the receiving end of that kind of love, thank God for it today.

*You don't choose your family.
They are God's gift to you, as you are to them.*

DESMOND TUTU

*You did not choose me, but I chose you and appointed you so
that you might go and bear fruit—fruit that will last—and so
that whatever you ask in my name the Father will give you.*

JOHN 15:16 NIV

*In the next year or so, my signature will appear on $60 billion
of United States currency. More important to me, however,
is the signature that appears on my life—the strong, proud,
assertive handwriting of a loving father and mother.*

KATHERINE D. ORTEGA
U.S. TREASURER

POWER UP

*How has love as or from a parent
shaped your relationship with God as your father?*

IT STARTS AT HOME

> *We need a better family life to make us*
> *better servants of the people.*
>
> **JIMMY CARTER**

It's true—how we love and live inside our homes spills out into how we love and serve others. Jesus reminds us in Matthew 22:39 to *"love your neighbor as yourself,"* but often, our first "neighbors" are the people under our own roof. When our families are rooted in love, grace, and respect, it becomes a foundation for how we treat the world around us. When that foundation is poorly built or damaged, everything built on top is bound to crumble under a facade of kindness. If you want to grow as a servant, begin with your own household and enjoy the blessing to follow.

*Spoil your husband, but don't spoil your children
—that's my philosophy.*

LOUISE SEVIER GIDDINGS CURREY
1961 NEW YORK POST MOTHER OF THE YEAR

*These commandments that I give you today are to be on your
hearts. Impress them on your children. Talk about them when
you sit at home and when you walk along the road, when you
lie down and when you get up.*

DEUTERONOMY 6:6-7 NIV

*President Johnson and I have a lot in common. We were both
born in small towns . . . and we're both fortunate in the fact
that we think we married above ourselves.*

RICHARD M. NIXON

POWER UP

*Do a household health checkup—
how is love, grace, and humility circulating in your home?*

A MASTERPIECE IN THE MAKING

The family is one of nature's masterpieces.

GEORGE SANTAYANA

F amily—a messy, beautiful, sometimes chaotic work of art that shapes us, teaches us, and reminds us we belong. No two families are alike and they are never perfect, but they are God's greenhouse for spiritual growth. Psalm 68:6 says, *"God sets the lonely in families."* That means whether it's biological, chosen, or spiritual family, He gives us people to walk alongside us. Be thankful for your masterpiece in progress that God is using to paint love and grace into your story.

Parents are the ultimate role models for children. Every word, movement and action has an effect. No other person or outside force has a greater influence on a child than the parent.

BOB KEESHAN

We love because he first loved us.

1 JOHN 4:19 NIV

There's nothing I value more than the closeness of friends and family, a smile as I pass someone on the street.

WILLIE STARGELL

POWER UP

How can you cherish and nurture your family with the same attention to detail as an artist?

THE ULTIMATE ADVENTURE

Bringing up a family should be an adventure.

MILTON R. SAPIRSTEIN

R aising a family isn't always neat, quiet, or predictable — but isn't that what makes it an adventure? There will be ups and downs, unexpected twists, and more than enough messes along the way, but God is writing a beautiful story through it all. Psalm 127:3 reminds us, "*Children are a heritage from the Lord, offspring a reward from him.*" Family life stretches us, grows us, and fills our hearts with moments we'll treasure forever — even on the hard days.

Our children are not going to be just "our children"—they are going to be other people's husbands and wives and the parents of our grandchildren.

MARY S. CALDERONE

But the mercy of the Lord is from everlasting to everlasting upon them that fear him, and his righteousness unto children's children . . .

PSALMS 103:17

A boy becomes an adult three years before his parents think he does and about two years after he thinks he does.

LEWIS B. HERSHEY

POWER UP

Are you approaching family life with a spirit of curiosity and joy, or have routine and stress stolen the sense of adventure?

ACTIONS SPEAK LOUDEST

*The best kind of parent you can be
is to lead by example.*

DREW BARRYMORE

K ids may not always listen to what we say, but you can bet they're always watching what we do. Whether it's how we handle stress, how we show kindness, or how we lean on God in tough moments, our actions speak loudest. Proverbs 20:7 says, "*The righteous lead blameless lives; blessed are their children after them.*" It doesn't mean being perfect—it means showing our kids how humility and perseverance are outworked in real life. Every day is a new chance to be the kind of example that points them down the path of godliness.

More than in any other human relationship, overwhelmingly more, motherhood means being instantly interruptible, responsive, responsible.

TILLE OLSEN

"Which of you fathers, if your son asks for a fish, will give him a snake instead? If you then, though you are evil, know how to give good gifts to your children, how much more will your Father in heaven give the Holy Spirit to those who ask him!"

LUKE 11:11,13 NIV

Friendship with oneself is all-important, because without it one cannot be friends with anyone else in the world.

ELEANOR ROOSEVELT

POWER UP

*What example would you like to set
for your children's best success in life?*

_____

_____

_____

_____

_____

THE POWER OF LAUGHTER

> *Once you get people laughing, they're listening and you can tell them almost anything.*
>
> **HERBERT GARDNER**

Laughter has a way of breaking down walls and opening hearts. Even Proverbs 17:22 reminds us, "*A cheerful heart is good medicine.*" When we approach life—and even tough conversations—with joy, kindness, and a little humor, people lean in and not away. It doesn't mean we take life lightly, but it does mean we bring light into life. Look for those moments to share a laugh, ease someone's heart, and let God use your joy to open doors for His love and truth.

A person reveals his character by nothing so clearly as the joke he resents.

G. C. LICHTENBERG

A merry heart doeth good like a medicine: but a broken spirit drieth the bones.

PROVERBS 17:22

Among those whom I like, I can find no common denominator, but among those whom I love, I can; all of them make me laugh.

W. H. AUDEN

POWER UP

How could you nurture joy and laughter in this season of life?

_____

_____

_____

_____

_____

NEW CONNECTIONS, NEW LIFE

It's easy to get comfortable with the people we know, but life has a beautiful way of bringing new faces across our path. God created us for community, and sometimes that means stepping out of our comfort zone to meet new people, hear new stories, and share our own. Every new friendship starts with a simple hello, a shared smile, or a moment of kindness. Keep your heart open—you never know who God might bring into your life to bless you . . . or who needs the blessing of knowing you!

When the character of a man is not clear to you,
look at his friends.

JAPANESE PROVERB

As iron sharpens iron, so one man sharpens another.

PROVERBS 27:17

The best time to make friends is before you need them.

ETHEL BARRYMORE

POWER UP

Are you open to new relationships and perspectives,
or have you grown too comfortable in familiar circles?

_____

_____

_____

_____

_____

WISDOM UNDER THE RADAR

People who carry wisdom with humility seem rare nowadays. Maybe they are quietly living among us, drowned out by voices eager for recognition. True wisdom doesn't need to shout to be heard; it shows up in how we live, how we love, and how we treat others. The Bible reminds us in Proverbs 27:2, "*Let someone else praise you, and not your own mouth.*" Today, let your life speak for itself. Quiet confidence, gentle words, and humble actions often teach more than a thousand lectures ever could.

Sometimes it's worse to win a fight than to lose.

BILLIE HOLIDAY

The wise prevail through great power, and those who have knowledge muster their strength.

PROVERBS 24:5 NIV

A friend can tell you things you don't want to tell yourself.

FRANCES WARD WELLER

POWER UP

Are you satisfied with quiet wisdom or do you have a desire for public recognition?

SEASONAL FRIENDSHIPS

> *A false friend and a shadow attend*
> *only while the sun shines.*
>
> BENJAMIN FRANKLIN

Everyone has had a "fair-weather friend". Jesus knows the pain of abandonment at hard times well. At Gethsemane, his disciples would not stay awake to watch and pray with him on the night of his arrest. When he was being beaten and hung on the cross, where were his crowds of devoted followers? All this and yet we see him extend nothing but forgiveness. Let's be inspired by his example of grace towards seasonal friends, and thank God for the ones who show up, stick around, and love through it all.

If you want to grow up, go up. Associate with people whose achievements exceed your own and model the growth you desire.

JOHN C. MAXWELL

Bless those who persecute you; bless and do not curse. Rejoice with those who rejoice; mourn with those who mourn.

ROMANS 12:14-15 NIV

No man is an island entire of itself; every man is a part of the continent, a part of the main.

JOHN DONNE

POWER UP

When challenges arise, who do you run to first?

_____

_____

_____

_____

_____

ABOUT THE AUTHOR

J ohn Maxwell is one of the world's most respected authorities on leadership and personal effectiveness. He has written more than a hundred books, including the *New York Times* best seller *The 21 Irrefutable Laws of Leadership*, which has sold more than 4 million copies. In addition to his writing career, he is a popular speaker, inspiring more than 250,000 people annually at appearances nationwide.

Dr. Maxwell's advice is based on his thirty-plus years of experience as a pastoral and organizational leader. He is founder of Maxwell Leadership, an organization that helps people maximize their personal and leadership potential. He has served as a senior pastor for churches in California, Ohio, Indiana, and Florida.

Dr. Maxwell lives in Atlanta, Georgia, with Margaret, his wife of more than fifty years.

Additional copies of this book and other titles
from Honor Books are available online.
Also available from this series:

The Power of Thinking Big
The Power of Leadership
The Power of Attitude
The Power of Influence